FASCINATING FOOD

FOOD DELIVERY

BY ALEXIS BURLING

Essential Library

An Imprint of Abdo Publishing
abdobooks.com

ABDOBOOKS.COM

Published by Abdo Publishing, a division of ABDO, PO Box 398166, Minneapolis, Minnesota 55439.

Printed in China.
102024
012025

THIS BOOK CONTAINS RECYCLED MATERIALS

Cover Photos: Richard A. Brooks/AFP/Getty Images (front); Shutterstock Images (back)
Interior Photos: Richard A. Brooks/AFP/Getty Images, 1; Tayfun Coskun/Anadolu Agency/Getty Images, 5; Lindsey Nicholson/UCG/Universal Images Group/Getty Images, 8; Laura Bonilla Cal/AFP/Getty Images, 12; English Heritage/Heritage Images/Hulton Archive/Getty Images, 15; H. Armstrong Roberts/ClassicStock/Archive Photos/Getty Images, 18–19; Universal History Archive/Universal Images Group/Getty Images, 20; Peter Morris/Fairfax Media Archives/Getty Images, 24; Michel Delsol/Archive Photos/Getty Images, 26–27; Red Line Editorial, 30, 44; Michael Macor/San Francisco Chronicle/Hearst Newspapers/Getty Images, 32; Jin Lee/Bloomberg/Getty Images, 34; Shutterstock Images, 39; Horacio Villalobos/Corbis News/Getty Images, 40; David L. Ryan/Boston Globe/Getty Images, 43; Theodore Parisienne/New York Daily News/Getty Images, 47; Andrew Lichtenstein/Corbis News/Getty Images, 50; Smith Collection/Gado/Archive Photos/Getty Images, 53; Rob Kim/Getty Images for NYCWFF/Getty Images Entertainment/Getty Images, 57; Lane Turner/Boston Globe/Getty Images, 58; Chance Yeh/Getty Images for NYCWFF/Getty Images Entertainment/Getty Images, 61; Daria Nipot/Shutterstock Images, 65, 76; Scott Eisen/Getty Images News/Getty Images, 68; Vivien Killilea/Getty Images for Gold House/Getty Images Entertainment/Getty Images, 73; Visual China Group/Getty Images, 79; Ezume Images/Shutterstock Images, 82; Brent Hofacker/Shutterstock Images, 85; Claudio Lucca/Shutterstock Images, 86; Tada Images/Shutterstock Images, 89; Prasit Rodphan/Shutterstock Images, 91; AaronP/Bauer-Griffin/GC Images/Getty Images, 94; Craig Barritt/Getty Images for Fast Company/Getty Images Entertainment/Getty Images, 97

Editor: Arnold Ringstad
Series Designer: Maggie Villaume

Library of Congress Control Number: 2024938294

PUBLISHER'S CATALOGING-IN-PUBLICATION DATA
Names: Burling, Alexis, author.
Title: Food delivery / by Alexis Burling
Description: Minneapolis, Minnesota: ABDO Publishing, 2025 | Series: Fascinating food | Includes online resources and index.
Identifiers: ISBN 9781098295264 (lib. bdg.) | ISBN 9798384916260 (ebook)
Subjects: LCSH: Food delivery services--Juvenile literature. | Store delivery services--Juvenile literature. | Delivery of goods--Juvenile literature. | Food industry and trade--Juvenile literature.
Classification: DDC 394.12--dc23

CONTENTS

CHAPTER ONE

BEING A DELIVERY DRIVER

Before 38-year-old William Medina moved to New York City in 2019, he had a good life in Bogotá, the capital of Colombia. He worked as a bank risk analyst at an insurance company, and he had lots of friends. When he relocated to be closer to his sisters and niece, he got a job as a deliverista, or delivery driver. "Many immigrants like me turn to delivery work because it is an accessible way to start making money for people new to the country with families they need to support," he said.[1]

Medina was excited to start his new job. Working as a deliverista meant he could have a certain amount of freedom to make his own schedule during the day, and he wouldn't have to wear fancy clothes to work as he did at his last job. Delivering food would also be an easy and convenient way to get to know the city. While zooming around buses, cars,

Delivering food on New York City's busy streets is a challenging and even dangerous job.

and pedestrians on his Yamaha Zuma 125 scooter, he could bring orders from restaurants to customers' homes and businesses in a flash.

But once he started, Medina quickly realized that there were many risks and demands that came with the job. Dense, never-ending traffic filled the New York City streets. To earn decent money, he would have to work many hours. Roads were filled with cars and trucks, which created safety hazards, especially in poor weather.

OUT-OF-POCKET COSTS

When people think of food delivery, the assumption may be that workers can just jump in the car they already own and go. But in New York City, where most deliveristas ride mopeds, bikes, or electric bikes to quickly navigate the busy streets, the cost of buying and maintaining that bike is the worker's responsibility. If a scooter is the vehicle of choice, workers must supply their own fuel, oil, helmet, and bike lock. They must pay for repairs in the case of an accident. If a bike gets stolen—which happens often in New York City—it's up to the worker to purchase a new ride.

He would have to stay focused. Medina had to keep his eye on his long-term goal of making a life for himself in his new city if he was going to get through the day in one piece and avoid burning out. "When I first started delivering, I learned that a disciplined work ethic is necessary to deal with the city's long list of challenges and dangers, from exploitative app companies to the constant threat of traffic crashes," he said.[2]

OVERWORKED AND UNDERPAID

Like many deliveristas in New York City, Medina kept a busy schedule in order to make the most money possible. For the next four years, even during the COVID-19 pandemic, he got up at the crack of dawn. This gave him enough time to connect to the food delivery apps, accept his first ride from one of the apps, and make his first delivery by 8:00 a.m. To maximize his profits, he delivered food for both DoorDash and Grubhub. These delivery platforms paid him by the order—a sum that he said amounted to about $4 per hour, before tips and after expenses.

In 2024, there were an estimated 65,000 food delivery workers in New York City.[4]

For Medina, a great day on the job was when he made 30 to 40 deliveries all over the borough of Queens, sometimes traveling hundreds of miles in a day. But that usually took him anywhere between ten and 14 hours, and he worked seven days a week.[3] He was physically and

Areas with many popular restaurants may have multiple delivery workers waiting nearby for new orders to come in.

mentally exhausted. “The pay structure created by delivery apps is set up so that most of the money a deliverista receives on an order comes from tips while the apps pay pennies on the dollar,” he said. “This leads deliveristas to put themselves in dangerous situations like using sidewalks and going at unsafe speeds so that we can make enough trips to make ends meet.”[5]

Despite his packed work schedule, Medina still felt as if he was always strapped for money. Like any food delivery worker, he didn’t qualify for health insurance from DoorDash or Grubhub, so he paid for any medical care out of pocket.

During the winter when roads were icy and he had to ride through rainstorms, snow, and sleet, the work felt especially grueling. "Winter usually pushes people indoors, causing people to order delivery more often, but that can be a double-edged sword: it provides us with more opportunities to make money, but in a city like New York, hazardous ice, snow, and freezing conditions can be a recipe for disaster," he said.[6]

Another challenge Medina faced was the constant threat to his safety. Though he never had his Yamaha stolen, bike theft was a persistent problem in the city. An estimated 54 percent of New York City deliveristas surveyed said they had been victims of bike theft. About 30 percent of delivery workers were physically assaulted during robberies.[7]

Other food couriers died on the job. From 2020 to 2022, 33 restaurant and app delivery workers were killed in traffic accidents while on duty.[8] "The threat of theft forces many vulnerable deliveristas into busy public spaces and onto well-lit roads, but these roads often have more dangerous car and truck traffic," Medina says. "It's a very stressful experience knowing our investments and means of work could be taken from us, and that the apps won't reimburse us if something happens."[9]

DANGEROUS DELIVERIES

According to 2023 data from the Bureau of Labor Statistics, working for ride sharing or food delivery services is among the most dangerous occupations in the United States. Workers face dangers such as robberies, traffic accidents, carjackings, physical attacks, and even homicides. In Florida, one DoorDash deliverista was kidnapped and sexually assaulted after bringing food to a guest at a hotel. Apps have implemented safety features, including an emergency button that's connected to a private security firm and a feature that transmits a worker's ID and location to emergency responders if the worker calls 911 while using the app.

A CALL TO ACTION

Medina said he was devoted to his job. But after a few years behind the handlebars, he felt it was increasingly important to start fighting for safer conditions and higher pay for delivery app workers. In 2020, he and his coworkers formed Los Deliveristas Unidos, an advocacy group representing delivery workers in New York City. People of many nationalities became members, include drivers from El Salvador, Venezuela, Colombia, Mexico, Bangladesh, China, and Nepal.

Hildalyn Colón Hernández, the director of policy for Los Deliveristas Unidos, said a pay raise was at the top of the group's agenda. During the pandemic, when the lockdown was in full swing, many drivers lost much of their income. One Mexican immigrant, a veteran deliverista who had made more than 4,000 deliveries for DoorDash, earned the equivalent of $20 a day—far less than the amount he'd need to eat and afford his rent. "We're fighting for the bare minimum. This is about their dignity," Hernández said. "Firefighters don't just get paid when they have a fire. They get paid for the time they are waiting in the firehouse for that call. We're asking for the same thing."[10]

In 2024, Medina was still living in New York City and working with Los Deliveristas Unidos and its parent group, the Worker's Justice Project, to secure better pay and conditions for delivery workers. He was married and spent as much of his time off as he could with his sisters and niece. He also continued to deliver food to hungry New Yorkers. "Being a deliverista means navigating a world of physical and mental challenges," he said. "At the

THE WORKER'S JUSTICE PROJECT

Formed in 2010, the Worker's Justice Project is an organization based in Brooklyn, New York, that seeks better, safer conditions in the workplace, greater pay and tip transparency, and expanded labor protections for app-based workers. It has thousands of members, many of whom are immigrants with jobs in construction, food delivery, or maid service. The Worker's Justice Project provides skills training and career coaching, and it teaches workers how to advocate for themselves through grassroots organizing.

Delivery drivers seeking to organize held a public meeting at Washington Square in New York City in June 2021.

end of the day, I am always proud of my work and even more proud that I get to work alongside inspiring people to change what we recognize to be unjust and unsafe, not just for us as workers, but for New York City as a whole."[11]

THE AGE OF FOOD DELIVERY

Medina is just one worker in a sea of people whose job it is to deliver food to hungry people in cities and towns across the world. Some people use apps such as DoorDash to order from restaurants. Others purchase foodie subscriptions such as the Cheese Explorer's Club from Murray's Cheese.

And some use meal delivery services such as Blue Apron that deliver ingredients and recipes, allowing people to easily prepare meals at home. Today's food delivery industry is larger than ever.

But having the culinary world at one's fingertips hasn't always been so easy or convenient. The tradition of getting food delivered has had a long and fascinating history. The story of food delivery spans continents and has been shaped by technological innovations ranging from horse-drawn carts to smartphones.

FOOD DELIVERY HISTORY

From cooking at home to dining in a restaurant to ordering food to go or having it delivered, the traditions around preparing and eating meals have evolved a lot over time. These days, getting food delivered in many places around the world is as easy as placing an order using a smartphone app. But long before modern technological advances, people had been enjoying food on the go in different parts of the world for hundreds of years.

EARLY FORMS OF DELIVERY

Historians are divided about which type of food was actually the first delivery on record and when that transaction took place. Butchers in Paris, France, for example, delivered prime cuts of meat to their wealthiest customers' homes as far back as the 1300s. In 1890s India, men called *dabbawalas*, which

Delivery of some foods and beverages, such as milk, dates back hundreds of years.

translates to "those who carry a box," traveled by bicycle or train to bring steaming-hot lunches in metal pails from various restaurants to workers in Mumbai and other large cities.

In the United States, food delivery dates back more than 200 years, when people got individual items such as flour or sugar delivered from a local shopkeeper or fresh milk dropped off from a nearby dairy farm. Before refrigerators became available for use at home in the early 1900s, large blocks of ice were transported in horse-drawn carriages from a local ice distributor to people's doors every day and stored in an ice box. Throughout US history, the food-delivery tradition has surprising connections to how the country has evolved over time.

In the early days of food delivery, many of the people who had access to this service were upper-class elites

WHAT'S A THERMOPOLIUM?

The convenience of food to go dates as far back as ancient Rome, when Romans could pick up a hot meal at a type of food stall called a thermopolium. It was usually a small room with an open-air front facing the street. Customers could line up in front of a stone counter and pick from a variety of hot or cold dishes stored in large clay containers, including lentils, eggs, meat or vegetable dishes, and olives. Some thermopolia had a small section of tables for eat-in dining, but most were takeout only. Many had brightly colored paintings on the walls or drawings of what dishes could be ordered from the menu.

who lived in urban areas. During the 1700s, fancy hotels advertised vacation packages to rich travelers. They could get a comfortable room or suite, plus any dish from a nearby restaurant delivered to their door at any time during their stay.

Whether it was a dozen freshly shucked oysters or a bowl of homemade ice cream, the arrangement benefited everyone involved. The restaurateur got paid. The hotel gained business after advertising the perk. And the hotel patron could enjoy tasty, locally made food in a comfortable setting throughout their vacation.

In the 1800s, catering companies in cities such as New York and Boston, Massachusetts, ran advertisements in local newspapers for lavish meals that could be picked up or delivered to homes. Renowned New York chef and pastry cook Mrs. Poppleton

GOT MILK?

Today, most people in the United States buy milk at their local supermarket. In the 1700s, many people got fresh milk from a local dairy farm delivered right to their doorstep. The first milk deliveries in the United States occurred in Vermont in 1785. A milkman traveled door-to-door with a barrel full of milk and filled jugs, buckets, or pails at each house along the way. In 1879, milk was delivered in sanitized glass bottles for the first time, making the delivery process easier for the milkman and keeping the milk fresher for longer for the customer.

In the 1800s, some bakeries in the United States began delivering their goods to local customers in horse-drawn carts.

promised diners options such as almond soup, lobster pudding, anchovy toast, and beef tongue. The 20th Century Food Company in New Haven, Connecticut, delivered breaded lamb chops, beef stew and dumplings, and corned beef hash to hungry customers.

But food delivery wasn't always just a custom of the wealthy. Over time, it became a habit of the working class too. For people with lesser means or those from rural areas who didn't have access to delivery, takeout was another

convenient way to eat food outside the confines of a restaurant when there wasn't time to cook at home. In many ways, it was an important stepping stone for people to get used to the idea of food delivery.

For example, after the US Civil War (1861–1865), when industrialization took over the United States, people began commuting farther to work, often from rural areas to the city. Construction workers, tradespeople, and other travelers picked up to-go lunch boxes from restaurants in train

Segregation in restaurants, including separate entrances for white people and people of color, lasted until the mid-1900s.

stations or at the intersections of major highways while on their way to their jobs. As the practice took off, many urban eateries started offering take-home dinner specials for workers to bring home to the family. Some even included delicacies such as oysters, scallops, and seafood chowder. Chas. Bradley's Oyster & Dining Room in New York City sold fried scallops in a box for 25 cents, while Sagamore Restaurant and Lunch Room advertised oyster stew in a can for 30 cents.

For Black travelers in the South, getting food to go from a store or restaurant wasn't just convenient, it was a necessity. In the late 1800s and early 1900s, discriminatory state and local laws called Jim Crow laws denied Black people equal rights and barred them from having any political representation. During this time, most stores and restaurants in the South and some in the North were segregated. This meant Black people weren't allowed to eat at the same dining establishments as whites—or they were allowed to eat only in the back. For this reason, takeout from the service entrances of stores and restaurants became a lifeline for Black travelers or workers searching for a hot meal on the road. Many times, it was the only way they could eat, especially if they were traveling long distances.

THE FIRST DELIVERIES

By the 1920s, many people in the United States had gotten used to takeout as a worthwhile alternative to eating in a restaurant or cooking a meal from scratch at home. They could pick up food from local restaurants and take it home themselves to eat. But in Los Angeles, California, a new type of service emerged that changed the course of culinary history: home food delivery.

In 1922, a Chinese restaurant called Kin-Chu Cafe ran ads saying it was "the only place on the West Coast making and delivering real Chinese dishes."[1] People were thrilled that the restaurant brought authentic dishes such as mapo tofu and

The Domino's Pizza chain, founded in 1960 in Ypsilanti, Michigan, promised that its pizza could be delivered to any local address in 30 minutes or less.[3]

kung pao chicken to their door, even as late as 1:00 a.m., and they placed orders from the establishment in droves.

In the years following World War II (1939–1945), more Americans bought cars and moved away from cities to the suburbs. Restaurant traffic in urban areas declined. Families began spending more time at home watching the newly invented television set, and restaurants started advertising carry-out or delivery menus full of dishes made for sitting and eating in front of the TV.

This move significantly boosted restaurants' profits. "By the end of [the 1950s] . . . restaurant food at home was no longer just for rich people or just for those without any other option," says Emelyn Rude, a reporter for *Time* magazine. "In the postwar years, takeout and delivery became something for everyone."[2]

One particularly popular takeout menu item was pizza. The *New York Times* even ran an article in 1944 devoted entirely to pizza, which was relatively new to the United States. It explained, "One of the most popular dishes in

Southern Italy, especially in the vicinity of Naples, is pizza—a pie made from a yeast dough and filled with any number of different centers, each one containing tomatoes. Cheese, mushrooms, anchovies, capers, onions, and so on may be used."[4]

In 1944, restaurants in New York City created a special cardboard box that was made especially for taking pizzas home. In 1952, a Los Angeles pizza parlor called Casa D'Amore began offering one of the first examples of free meal delivery in the United States. Customers could order a medium pizza for just $2.25, add some drinks or a side salad, and get the whole thing delivered right to their home at no extra cost.

Senior citizens and some disabled veterans from World War II benefited from this delivery trend too. In 1954, Meals on Wheels—an

A LEGENDARY PIZZA

By the mid-1900s, food delivery had become common in many places all over the world, but legend has it that two people got to enjoy fresh pizza at home more than 100 years ago in Italy. In 1889, Italian king Umberto I and queen Margherita of Savoy were visiting Naples and wanted to try food prepared by famous local pizza maker Raffaele Esposito. In total, Esposito delivered three pizzas to the royals' quarters. Queen Margherita's favorite resembled the Italian flag, with red tomato sauce, white cheese, and clippings of green basil leaves. This style of pizza is still called Margherita to this day.

Domino's Pizza workers in the 1980s took orders by phone, prepared the pizzas, and drove them to customers' houses.

organization in the United Kingdom that provides free meals to older people in need—made its first US food delivery in Philadelphia, Pennsylvania. Today, the group delivers millions of meals each year to seniors in communities across the country.

Well into the 1980s, the food delivery phenomenon continued to hold steady and remained popular with the public. Domino's Pizza and other chains hired an army of part-time delivery drivers to keep up with the demand for pizza. But in the years leading up to the turn of the millennium, a new invention called the internet changed food delivery forever.

CHAPTER THREE

THE INTERNET CHANGES EVERYTHING

By the late 1980s and early 1990s, food delivery was popular in big cities and medium-sized towns across the United States—especially in the suburbs. Companies such as Takeout Taxi, Gourmet Express, Dinners to Go, and Cuisine on Call delivered food from local restaurants in various parts of the country. This made it easier for parents in dual-income households to work a full day and then go home to take care of the kids and not have to worry about cooking dinner.

"In the 1950s and 60s, Mom had as her full-time job raising the children. Now it's Mom with a full-time job and Dad with a full-time job and the two of them sharing a third full-time job, which is raising the family," Kevin Abt told the *New York Times* in 1992. He was the chairman and founder of Takeout Taxi Franchising Systems. "It's highly unlikely Mom is going to retreat back into the home,

The advent of widespread personal computers and home internet connections by the early 1990s opened up new possibilities for food delivery.

so both parents are going to need as much additional help as they can get with that third job."[1]

The type of food available for delivery had expanded beyond Chinese and pizza too. From sushi rolls or grilled shrimp to a bucket of fried chicken or a rib eye steak, there seemed to be virtually limitless options. Customers got to try new types of food they might not normally cook at home, while the delivery companies took a portion of each check for their own profit.

Aside from making money on the order itself, restaurants saved money by being able to cut back on waitstaff and things such as tablecloths and napkins that delivery orders didn't require. "It doesn't matter if your customer is sitting in your restaurant or at home. They still purchased your food," explained Wendy Webster, a spokeswoman for the National Restaurant Association, in 1992.[2]

Then, just as food delivery seemed to be at its peak, a new phenomenon turned the entire food-ordering process on its head once again. In the 1980s and 1990s, more families could afford to buy personal computers, and home internet connections became more widespread. People could now order food to be delivered to their homes or offices using the internet instead of a telephone.

A DIGITAL REVOLUTION

One of the earliest e-commerce companies was an online platform for grocery delivery. In 1989, brothers Andrew and Thomas Parkinson started a new company called Peapod out of their garage in Evanston, Illinois. Peapod's early customers throughout Chicago, Illinois, could put together a grocery list of desired items using the company's software.

The Parkinson brothers would then go to the closest local supermarket, handpick the groceries and load them into their van, and then deliver them to the customer. "We wanted to fundamentally improve people's lives by making it easier to shop," says Andrew Parkinson. "We did that by bringing an interactive shopping experience to a broad customer market."[3]

Five years after Peapod's launch, the first website dedicated to delivering

EARLY ONLINE FOOD DELIVERY WORLDWIDE

The United States had early innovators in the online food delivery experience, but other parts of the world got in on the game too. In 2000, food delivery company Yemeksepeti launched in Turkey and soon expanded across the Middle East to countries such as the United Arab Emirates, Saudi Arabia, Lebanon, Oman, Qatar, and Jordan. That same year, Takeaway.com was founded by foodie entrepreneur Jitse Groen in Amsterdam, the Netherlands. The company later merged with the food delivery service Just Eat. By 2024, the combined company was still going strong.

Pizza Hut's original PizzaNet website was far simpler than the flashy websites and apps used for food delivery today.

restaurant food was born. In 1994, the chain Pizza Hut created a platform called PizzaNet. This made it quicker and easier for consumers to get a fresh pizza.

As part of PizzaNet's initial launch, people in Santa Cruz, California, could browse a menu online, choose the type of pizza and toppings they wanted, and press a button to order. The order would be transmitted over a phone line to a centralized Pizza Hut server in Wichita, Kansas, and then to the closest Pizza Hut in Santa Cruz, whose staff would make the delivery. "The point is, what we want to do is make it fun to order and have fun with it and turn our product into a service," said Pizza Hut's Jon Payne at the time. "I suspect there will be some element of entertainment involved to make this thing really go. . . . I expect to get a lot of creative ideas over the Internet about what we should do next."[4]

Hot on the heels of PizzaNet's launch, another food delivery website popped up on the internet in 1995, this one featuring an array of menus from a few different restaurants. Created by Michael Adelberg and Craig Cohen, World Wide Waiter (later changed to Waiter.com) served residents of the San Francisco Bay Area in California. Users could order food from dozens of local restaurants for delivery or takeout. The types of food available included Japanese, Thai, Caribbean, Mexican, and more.

Little by little, especially with the help of local and national media coverage, the concept of ordering food online caught on. Throughout the 1990s and into the early 2000s, other delivery services appeared. Some found success, but most of them eventually flopped.

In 1996, shoppers in San Francisco started using a new company called Webvan for grocery delivery. In 1997, a similar service called HomeGrocer.com joined the scene. Webvan bought the company in 2000 and went bankrupt in 2001.

In 1998, the on-demand delivery company Kozmo began bringing products such as video games, DVDs, and even a single pack of gum to customers' doorsteps. Every delivery was guaranteed in about an hour. "The one disadvantage that e-commerce has versus shopping in a physical store is instant gratification, at least for physical products," said

Webvan's stock price topped out at more than $25 per share in December 1999. By July 2001, when the company went out of business, its share price had dropped to $0.06.

Kozmo cofounder Joseph Park at the time. "Today, it's still a compelling idea that you could get all the benefits of online shopping and combine that with one of the most important aspects of offline shopping: getting your merchandise immediately."[5] The company was an overnight sensation, but it shut down just a few years later in 2001.

A SEAMLESS TRANSITION

One of the biggest developments in the online food delivery scene took place in December 1999. A New York City lawyer named Jason Finger cofounded SeamlessWeb (later changed to Seamless). The website connected the workers at the city's law firms and investment banks with restaurants and caterers in their neighborhood.

"I was working as an associate at a New York law firm and we would work late, so I would collect everyone's takeout orders. . . . One Thanksgiving I was about to take orders and couldn't find restaurants that were open, so I worked with my co-founders to come up with the idea of starting a company with Web-enabled menus," Finger says. "The whole idea centered on making it easier for companies to enter in food budget restrictions. Employees could then order and the restaurant would charge the company, [eliminating] any need for employee reimbursement."[6]

Word about the ease of Seamless spread slowly but steadily. Over the next couple of years, the concept became so popular with businesses

ROAMING HUNGER

In 2009, Los Angeles resident Ross Resnick took a major risk. He used his life savings of $3,000 to start a company and build a website called Roaming Hunger. The site allows users to track all the street food vendors, food carts, and food trucks in their city. At first, Resnick started small, with 300 food trucks. By 2024, the site listed more than 18,000 of the best food trucks, carts, and caterers in the country. "From backyard birthdays to large-scale festivals, we've helped thousands of hosts and vendors connect to provide food service, catering and branded food truck promotions," Resnick says.[7]

Grubhub was listed on the New York Stock Exchange in April 2014, raising nearly $200 million from investors.

in New York City that other sites started cropping up to serve noncorporate markets. In 2004, two web developers in Chicago named Matt Maloney and Mike Evans founded Grubhub, a site similar to Seamless but geared toward everyday consumers. A year later, Seamless expanded its formerly corporate-only website to members of the public.

Over the next decade, a slew of other online restaurant delivery sites emerged, including DoorDash, Caviar, and Postmates. Some were successful. Others, including Dotmenu, Allmenus, and MenuPages, either were acquired by larger services or couldn't compete and shut down.

INVESTMENT AND GROWTH

By 2014, online delivery seemed to be the hottest trend in the culinary market, with venture capitalists investing a lot of money in the field. Just a year prior, Seamless had merged with Grubhub, creating a juggernaut in the industry. The combined company went on to acquire other regionally popular sites, including Foodler and Eat24.

Another soon-to-be delivery giant, Uber Eats, was founded in Los Angeles in 2014. It was a new division of the ride-sharing platform Uber, which allowed people to earn money by giving rides to others. Uber Eats expanded this concept to food delivery. Within just a few years, Uber Eats racked up billions in sales, recruited a vast number of new delivery drivers, and brought its operations to dozens of countries around the world.

By 2020, the food-delivery landscape had transformed once again, this time thanks to the adoption of dedicated delivery apps for smartphones, which made the process of ordering food even easier, especially for people on the go. By March 2020, 38 percent of Americans had ordered food using a delivery app.[8] Millions of people were spending billions of dollars per year on food delivery in the United States. And the trend showed no signs of slowing down.

THE PANDEMIC AND FOOD DELIVERY

Then something happened that no one saw coming, affecting the food delivery market more than anything had ever before. In early 2020, the infectious disease COVID-19 spread around the world. Millions of people died, and governments asked people to stay home and avoid contact with others to stop the pandemic's spread.

In 2024, more than 800,000 restaurants were available on Uber Eats in 11,000 cities around the world.[9]

Many businesses and schools closed during the pandemic. Restaurants closed too, with some transitioning to delivery only. The pandemic affected all aspects of society and had devastating consequences. But food delivery services actually benefited. Because they gave people a way to get their favorite restaurant meals while minimizing the risk of catching COVID-19, the popularity of these services exploded.

The four largest food-delivery companies in the United States are DoorDash, Grubhub, Uber Eats, and Postmates. Together, they earned about $5.5 billion in revenue between April and September 2020. That was more than twice their combined $2.5 billion in revenue during the same months in 2019.[10] In the following years, the revenue for online food delivery in the United States kept moving upward. In 2024, economists projected the industry's total revenue would reach more than $500 billion by 2029.[11]

PANDEMIC RESTAURANT CLOSURES

During the COVID-19 pandemic, restaurants worldwide struggled to stay afloat. According to a National Restaurant Association impact survey, eight million restaurant employees in the United States had lost their jobs by April 20, 2020.[12] By the end of that year, more than 110,000 restaurants and bars had either temporarily or permanently closed. Of those restaurants that closed permanently, about 16 percent had been running for at least 30 years.[13]

CHAPTER FOUR

CONTROVERSIAL APPS

When food delivery apps such as Grubhub, Uber Eats, and DoorDash first appeared on the scene in the early 2000s, many saw them as a win for restaurants, consumers, and the app companies themselves. They attracted new and repeat customers for restaurants, provided more food options for consumers, and generated revenue for the delivery app companies. The way the business arrangement worked was simple. The tech company charged a fee—sometimes more than 40 percent of the total—for every order the restaurant got.[1] In most cases, the tech company also charged customers a fee for each delivery.

Over time, especially during the COVID-19 pandemic when many people and business owners were struggling to stay afloat, restaurants and even the people who worked for the delivery apps began

The widespread adoption of smartphones and apps made it easier than ever for people to place food delivery orders from a variety of services.

Food delivery apps profited enormously from the rising popularity of food delivery during the COVID-19 pandemic.

to see that this arrangement was far from ideal. It seemed as if the only clear winners were the tech companies behind the apps. From steep fees to low wages to communication issues, it became clear that working with these delivery apps could create more problems than benefits. "Many restaurants are realizing that they're taking a loss on every order through the delivery apps, so those orders don't make economic sense," *New York Times* reporter Nathaniel Popper wrote in 2020. "Beyond the fees, many restaurants said they felt that delivery apps weren't good partners—they found it difficult, for example, to reach delivery services to fix problems."[2]

HIGH FEES

After going into business with delivery apps, restaurant owners quickly realized that the fees associated with delivery services ate into their profits. This put a major dent in their bottom line. In many cases, these restaurants had to raise prices or reduce portion sizes to offset the fees charged by delivery platforms. The public wasn't happy about the rise in prices of menu items, so many people decided to cut back on ordering food for delivery. This hurt restaurants even more.

Despite this strain on finances, many restaurant owners felt pressure to remain in business with delivery app companies—especially during the pandemic. Because no one was eating in restaurants during the lockdowns, orders through food delivery apps were the only way for restaurants to make money. Still, on top of paying rent, buying ingredients, and paying staff, many restaurant proprietors barely had any money left over to keep their establishments running. With tech companies taking a large chunk of their profits, they were making little money and felt stuck.

"You have no choice but to sign up, but there is no negotiating," says Matt Majesky, who ran a restaurant called Pierogi Mountain in Columbus, Ohio, and had partnered with Grubhub until the pandemic hit. A few months into the COVID-19 lockdowns, he had to shut down and apply for unemployment. "It almost turns into a hostage situation," he says.[3]

In June 2020, spending at restaurants dropped by 35 percent from the same time a year prior, while revenue for apps such as Uber Eats, Postmates, and Grubhub rose by 140 percent.[4] Like Majesky, restaurant owners across the country felt the pinch. Some lodged complaints or tried to start a grassroots anti-app movement on social media. Others cut their ties with the apps altogether and looked for different ways to do business.

"Everyone is trying to help us—our landlord, New York City, our customers," says New York restaurant owner George Constantinou. He did business with DoorDash, Uber Eats, and Grubhub. "But these companies who are supposed to be our partners take more money than anyone else and try to get us on every charge they can."[5]

The closure of dining rooms during the COVID-19 pandemic forced restaurants to rely more heavily on takeout and delivery for income.

US FOOD DELIVERY APP MARKET SHARE[6]

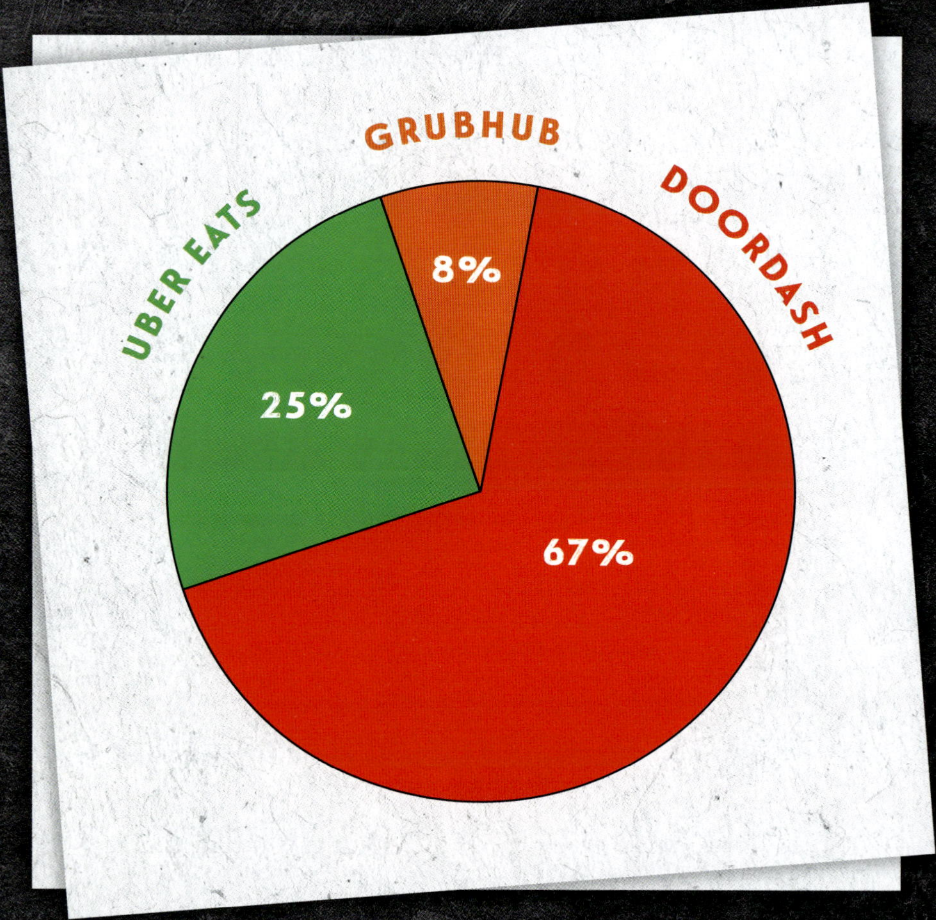

In 2023, three companies dominated the US food delivery app market, with DoorDash being by far the largest.

In response to the complaints, cities across the United States enacted legislation or emergency rules to cap the apps' fees until the lockdowns were over. Washington, DC; Seattle, Washington; Los Angeles; New York City; and San Francisco capped the fees at 15 percent. Hoboken and Jersey City in New Jersey capped fees at 10 percent. Since March 2020, four states have passed fee caps for all their cities and counties: Massachusetts and Washington at 15 percent, Oregon at 5 percent, and New Jersey at 20 percent and 10 percent, depending on the location.[7]

"People realized [during the pandemic], 'Oh, all these restaurants that we love and that have really, really low margins are being beat up by these Silicon Valley apps,' and legislators and the public really rallied around them,"

FAKE WEBSITES

In addition to lodging complaints about fees during the pandemic, some restaurants asserted food delivery apps were setting up fake websites containing incorrect information without the restaurants' permission. In 2020, a Denver, Colorado, restaurant chain called Freshcraft sued Grubhub, saying the company created websites that stated some of their locations were either closed or no longer taking orders—both false claims. "The fact that they misrepresented my brand in these times, and pushed Grubhub clients toward other restaurants—it's deplorable," said Freshcraft owner Erik Riggs.[8]

says Moe Tkacik, a senior fellow at the American Economic Liberties Project, a group that works against corporate monopolies. "It's conventional wisdom now that these companies are bloodsucking middlemen. They are really greedy, and they've hired a lot of fancy spin doctors, but it's just not that complicated an issue."[9]

LOW PAY, UNSAFE CONDITIONS

Restaurant owners weren't the only people with complaints about food delivery apps. The delivery workers themselves had to deal with what they said were unfair and unsafe working conditions throughout their workday. The way the food delivery business is set up, many of the drivers for delivery services are officially classified as independent contractors. This means they can't get benefits such as health insurance and paid time off as regular employees do.

In some cases, this has led to legal challenges and protests by delivery drivers, who argue that they should be classified as employees. "These apps are not only controlling the lives and the health of these workers but also determining who works and who has the ability to work," says Ligia Guallpa, executive director of the Worker's Justice Project. "They claim that these workers are independent

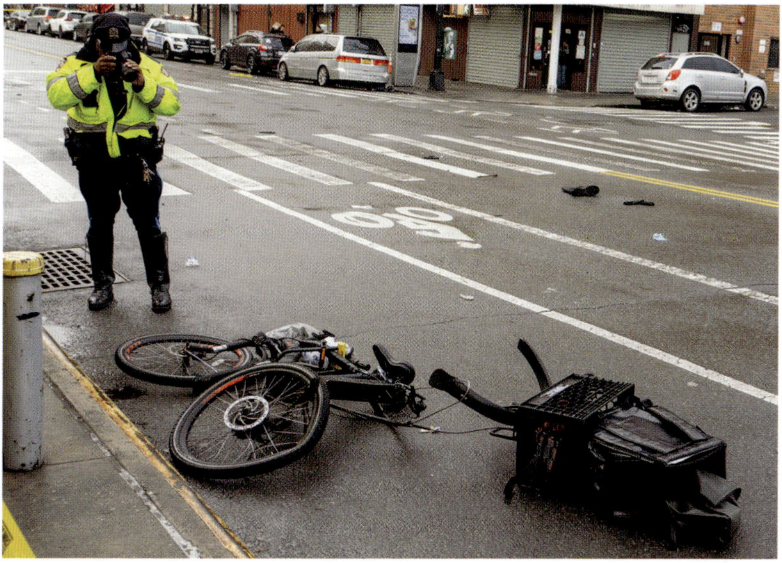

Delivering food on a bicycle or scooter is a dangerous job, and many workers have been injured or killed.

contractors but treat them as workers by determining how many hours they work, how many deliveries they make, and by not giving control of how much they earn."[10]

Some delivery workers say they also feel unsafe with the number of orders they have to run through, often on bikes in traffic. They say there aren't enough on-the-job protections in place to ensure their safety. For example, a food delivery worker in New York City in 2021 could make $400 to $500 per week delivering for DoorDash and Relay, another local company. In bad-weather weeks, when more customers stayed home and ordered food delivery, that number was closer to $800. But a worker could make

STOLEN TIPS

On top of low wages and a lack of health insurance, some workers reported that food delivery apps had been stealing their tips. In November 2020, the Washington, DC, attorney general reached a $2.5 million settlement with DoorDash over wage theft. This included $1.5 million in compensation to delivery drivers who reported they never received their tips. "Wage theft has happened to me and to some of the other workers," one worker said at the time. "I have confronted the apps when I noticed my tips were stolen. When I complain right away, they give the money back and say it was a system problem."[13]

that much only if they worked six days a week for ten hours a day.[11] The more orders these workers delivered, the more they made, but the more exhausted they felt—with no access to health insurance.

"Things were somewhat better before because at least we had an employer and had a set schedule," says Gustavo Ajche, a delivery worker who once worked directly for a restaurant but who later joined DoorDash. "The stability that existed between the restaurant and the workers is gone now. No matter how busy it was we still got paid by the hour. With the apps, you're paid only when you make a delivery. If there is no delivery, there is no money."[12]

As with many low-paying jobs, these types of problems fall mostly on people of color and immigrants, especially in big cities such as Los Angeles, San Francisco, Chicago, and New York City. "It's important to understand that these workers who have been feeding New York during the pandemic are mostly immigrant workers and that these apps not only disrupted the employee-employer relationship but have also been profiting from the labor of immigrant workers who [were] left without economic relief to survive the pandemic," says Guallpa.[14]

WHAT'S BEING DONE

After the federal public health emergency for COVID-19 officially ended in May 2023, dining inside restaurants came back in full swing. By 2024, restaurants were in much better shape financially than they had been just a few years earlier. For this reason, many restaurant owners have steered clear of the delivery apps altogether, preferring to staff in-house delivery drivers in order to retain control over their revenue.

Some cities, including Seattle and New York City, have enacted laws that would require the apps to pay delivery workers a higher hourly rate. A portion of this would cover workers' expenses. Wages would also include a little extra because these workers don't have workers' compensation insurance.

Beginning in 2023, app companies in Seattle had to pay per-minute and per-mile rates to delivery drivers. In New

In 2022, US representative Alexandria Ocasio-Cortez was among those celebrating the passage of New York City legislation protecting delivery drivers.

York City, new rules said workers would be paid an average hourly rate of at least $23.82, not including tips, by 2025.[15] This minimum rate would pertain to a delivery worker's "total trip time" each week, which is the amount of time between when a worker accepts an order and the time that order is delivered. It includes any traffic delays, the time it takes to wait for orders to come in, the time it takes to drive or ride to the restaurant, and the time it takes to wait for the order to be cooked.

Despite these advancements, many workers' rights advocates say there's still more to be done. But it's a start. "At the end of the day, it's about improving workers' lives and making sure their day-to-day is a little bit more tolerable," says Brian Chen, a senior staff lawyer for the National Employment Law Project, a nonprofit advocacy and research group.[16]

CONTINUING CHALLENGES

After the minimum pay rate for delivery workers went up in some cities around the United States, many workers rejoiced that they were finally getting the treatment and compensation they deserved. Others insisted the win was not as generous as it first seemed. In the weeks and months after the rules went into effect, some delivery drivers noticed that apps such as Uber Eats had removed the tip button from the app or made it more difficult to find.

CHAPTER FIVE

FOOD SUBSCRIPTIONS

For more than a century, diners have been able to get meals delivered to their homes. But these days, food from restaurants isn't the only thing people can get delivered. Diners can now get a full range of culinary products delivered to them through the mail using subscription services. All they have to do is go online to a website or an app, choose a subscription, and enter their credit card and address and they'll receive food in the mail on a regular basis.

These subscriptions have become a popular gift option too, especially during times when prices for goods are high and the economy is unstable. In 2023, for example, when inflation was on the rise and people were cutting back on spending, more people—especially younger people in the Gen Z and millennial generations—looked to subscription

The Universal Yums subscription box delivers a monthly assortment of snacks from various countries.

At the start of the pandemic in 2020, consumers who paid for subscription box services spent an average of $75 on food and meal kit services per month.[3]

services as a way to send a thoughtful gift on a budget.

In a 2023 survey of 1,000 people in the United States, two-thirds of respondents said they "definitely" or "possibly" were interested in giving a subscription as a gift during the holiday season.[1] Food and beverage subscriptions were the most popular. "Food has an innate ability to foster connections and bring people together," says Merilee Kern, host of the TV show *Savvy Living.* She explains,

> *Gastronomic subscriptions are not only gifts; they are vessels of shared, boundary-crossing experiences. Givers are not merely presenting a box of goodies, but rather are gifting moments of joy, discovery and joint indulgence. This communal aspect further enhances the appeal of food and beverage subscriptions as meaningful and memorable gifts.*[2]

A WORLD OF CHOICES

For eaters looking to do a little traveling during their meals, Try the World is a popular choice recommended by customers and food industry reporters alike. Each box participants receive is themed for a different country around the world, containing savory snacks and sugary treats from that country. Featured countries have included India, Brazil, and Spain. "Anyone with a sense of culinary wanderlust should check out Try the World," reads one article on the website Tastemade. "It's much cheaper than airfare."[4]

If people are interested specifically in snacks from Japan, they can try Bokksu. This service sends members a box packed with items such as seaweed tempura, green tea and lemon cakes, yuzu-flavored gummies, and matcha-strawberry Kit-Kats. Write-ups about the products are also included in the box to inform recipients about the treats' cultural or historical significance.

The legendary Levain Bakery in New York City has a monthly cookie subscription that mails eight massive cookies to dessert lovers' doors. Flavors include dark chocolate peanut butter chip, caramel coconut chocolate chip, and black-and-white chocolate chip. The subscription costs more than $40 per month, which may seem like a lot for a handful of cookies. But many devoted fans say it's worth it. The website Insider says, "I just seriously just don't see yet how any cookie could compare to this."[5]

A SUBSCRIPTION BOX FOR THE SWEET TOOTH

For people who have money to spare and a hankering for mouthwatering ice cream in interesting flavors, Salt & Straw of Portland, Oregon, has a subscription box that ships five pints through the mail. Options include a mix of seasonal flavors, Salt & Straw's bestsellers, or dairy-free pints every three months, six months, or 12 months. The flavors, such as pistachio with saffron and rose water, maraschino cherry with rainbow marshmallow fluff, and jasmine milk tea almond stracciatella, are varieties not found in most supermarkets.

For foodies looking for more niche products, there are plenty of subscription options that cater to their needs. RawSpiceBar sends two ounces (57 g) of a freshly ground single spice or a spice blend such as Indian garam masala or Japanese furikake. Fuego Box ships various bottles of hot sauce from around the country. Customers may receive just one bottle, or they can pay a higher price for the "Pain Seeker"—a box specifically geared toward people who like extra-hot sauces.

Fulton Fish Market is a legendary fishmonger in New York City. It offers subscription boxes for seafood lovers. "Everything I've ever ordered from Fulton Fish Market online has been fresh, and when you're talking seafood that's about as important as it gets," says CNET reporter David Watsky.[6]

Other food-based subscription services include those for premium and farm-raised beef, cheese, olive oil, bread and

New York City's Levain Bakery has a handful of locations mostly on the East Coast, but its subscription service brings its famous cookies to fans around the world.

other grains, pickles, oysters, and even soup dumplings. But not all food-based subscriptions are created equal, say the subscription testers at the website Serious Eats. This means it's important to research the details before buying.

"The best subscription boxes should be packaged with care: They shouldn't arrive broken or otherwise damaged because of a lack of padding," says Serious Eats reporter Riddley Gemperlein-Schirm. "If the item is chilled or frozen, it should come to your doorstep that way, too. The subscription site's website should be easy to navigate

Some restaurants, including Oleana in Cambridge, Massachusetts, offer meal delivery subscriptions to local customers.

and allow you to intuitively toggle between delivery frequencies, if applicable."[7]

DRINK SUBSCRIPTIONS

There are plenty of coffee and tea subscriptions for fans of hot beverages. For tea drinkers, Tea Runners mails a variety of tea in gift boxes. For coffee, Serious Eats commerce writer Jesse Raub, who spent 15 years in the specialty coffee industry, recommends Trade Coffee for people who don't know which type of coffee to pick. The monthly service begins with a quiz and then curates a selection of caffeinated or decaf coffee based on the participant's answers. The recommendations take into account brewing method (pour over, automatic drip, espresso machine) and roast preferences (dark, medium, light).

Fans of sparkling drinks can get in on the fun too. Root Beer Club sends out a frosty 12 pack every month to subscribers. Members can choose from a cream soda pack or a curated selection of 12 unique bottles of root beer from around the world. Aura Bora runs a flavor-of-the-month subscription option for people who just can't get enough

A SMOOTH WAY TO DRINK DAILY VITAMINS

Many people believe that drinking smoothies is a tasty way to get important vitamins and minerals. The SmoothieBox monthly subscription delivers freezer-ready smoothie concoctions. Each packet contains a mixture of organic fruits and vegetables without any added sugar or artificial sweeteners. Boxes include customizable flavor choices, such as chocolate, orange, and berry. "I love that SmoothieBox's products use organic produce, helping to minimize exposure to pesticides," says nutritionist Christina Badaracco. "They also include nuts or seeds that add healthy fats and protein and help to keep blood sugar stable."[8]

of drinking seltzer water. Selections include unusual flavors, such as peach honeysuckle, mango chili, and blueberry wildflower.

KITCHEN EQUIPMENT SUBSCRIPTIONS

Beyond specific foods and drinks, there are other types of subscriptions that help ensure every at-home chef or beginning cook can make the most out of their time in the kitchen. CrateChef is a subscription service curated by foodies around the world. Each month, a chef, cookbook author, cooking show star, restaurateur, recipe developer, or food blogger will pick out a few of their favorite food-related items and gadgets to include in the box.

Past items have included a baker's favorite spatula, a chef's most recent cookbook, measuring spoons, candles, and much more. Suggested recipes are sent along with each subscription. The box also includes a biography card of that month's curator and their inspirations for each item.

Former Oregon Commission for the Blind instructor and current chef Debra Erickson launched the Blind Kitchen. The company is dedicated to teaching people how to cook after vision loss. The Blind Kitchen has four different subscription

Molly Yeh is among the chefs whose work has been featured in CrateChef subscription boxes.

boxes full of adaptive tools catered specifically to visually impaired cooks.

The "Kitchen Basics" box helps cooks create a safe, more efficient work area with tools including a talking kitchen scale and an auto-measure spout. The "Stovetop" and "Oven Collection" boxes each contain adaptive tools to help visually impaired chefs safely navigate heated areas in the kitchen. A fourth box contains items such as a finger guard and a butter slicer to help blind cooks learn how to chop and slice without any cutting mishaps.

In addition to shipping these boxes, Erickson posts instructional videos online. They feature details on how to use each tool as well as a few specialized cooking strategies. "I feel that if

RECIPES BY MAIL

For people interested in the history of cooking or those who don't have enough space for 20 cookbooks, a monthly subscription to Recipes by Mail is a great gift. Subscribers receive replicas of handwritten recipes from historical figures such as Eleanor Roosevelt, Emily Dickinson, and George Washington. A write-up featuring the biographical and historical background of each recipe is included, along with notes about the significance and inspiration for the recipe. "If you've got a friend who loves flipping through cookbooks, but is quickly running out of shelf space—or a friend who's interested in both history and cooking—they're going to be obsessed with this," say Epicurious reporters Megan Wahn and Carina Finn.[9]

vision-impaired home cooks are provided with the right tools and information, they will have the same experience I did: pure joy at being able to provide family and friends with delicious and nutritious meals to nourish their bodies and their hearts," says Erickson.[10]

CHAPTER SIX

A RETURN TO COOKING

Given the popularity of food delivery apps and subscription services, it's more possible than ever to live in an apartment or house and eat food from a restaurant every night of the week. But what about busy people who appreciate trying a variety of cuisines but like to eat home-cooked food? Or those who prefer to prepare their own meals instead of getting takeout but just don't know how?

That's where meal kits come in. These ready-to-make food subscription services deliver a complete meal with all the prechopped and premeasured ingredients. Also included are a step-by-step recipe, an ingredient list with nutritional breakdowns, and plenty of how-to photos. New cooks and experienced chefs alike can get the enjoyment of preparing their own meals without all the fuss of searching for the right recipe,

With ingredients separately packaged and portioned, subscription meal kits make cooking a fresh meal relatively quick and easy.

shopping for the ingredients, and doing all the cutting and slicing. Plus, the meal kits don't require any tools aside from basics that are probably already in the kitchen, such as a pot or a knife. As far as ingredients, people usually need to provide only a handful of staples, such as salt, pepper, sugar, oil, or butter.

Overall, meal kit subscription services are designed to make meal planning easier and reduce the reliance on frequent trips to the grocery store. "Cooking dinner is a cinch with the best meal kit delivery services," says Kelly Woo, an editor for the website Tom's Guide. "With a few clicks on an app or website, you can order meal kits that bring you chef-prepared recipes with fresh, high quality ingredients. Just follow the instructions to whip up delicious meals from a variety of cuisines in less than an hour."[1]

Most meal delivery kits start with an entry-level subscription plan that serves two people with a specified number of meals per week. Larger plans are available for those with bigger families. The exact number of meals ordered and the types of ingredients—including options such as pork-free, gluten-free, and pescatarian—can be customized depending on the customer's needs. Depending on where they live, people can order meal kit subscriptions from a variety of companies, some of them major corporations and others smaller start-ups.

THE TOP TWO

There are many meal kit services available, including Home Chef, Sunbasket, Marley Spoon, and Dinnerly. The two largest are HelloFresh and Blue Apron. In 2022, HelloFresh was the most popular provider in the United States. In that year, it accounted for more than 70 percent of the meal kit market.[2] HelloFresh got its start in Germany in 2011. By the following year, it had spread to the United Kingdom, the Netherlands, and Austria. In 2013, HelloFresh hit the US market and continued to expand to other countries from there. In 2024, the company had more than 20,000 employees and 12,000 recipes in its database, including hoisin honey shrimp and roasted veggie kale salad with steak.[3]

The market value of the worldwide meal kit industry is projected to exceed $25 billion by 2027.[4]

While HelloFresh has a global reach, the next biggest meal kit company, Blue Apron, is available only in the contiguous United States. The company was founded in

Insulated packing materials keep the perishable ingredients in meal kits fresh during transit.

2012 in New York City. Customers could choose how many meals they wanted to receive each week. The idea took off, and the company expanded its offerings.

In 2014, Blue Apron opened an online market selling spice blends and various kitchen tools. In 2015, the company released its first mobile app so customers could pick out their meals on the go. Over the next few years, the company launched Blue Apron Wine, which delivered chef-recommended bottles of wine to go with each meal; a Blue Apron cookbook; and a test kitchen where chefs could try out recipes before including them in the Blue Apron catalog. In 2022, Blue Apron generated more than $450 million in sales.[5]

More than a decade after the company began, many reviewers rate Blue Apron as one of the best meal kit options available. "Which meal kit has the best food for the best price?" asks reporter David Watsky of CNET. "After more than 60 hours of cooking kits, heating prepared meals, and taking lots of notes, Blue Apron tops this list as the best meal kit service overall. Blue Apron recipes mostly take less than 30 minutes, and the standard menu includes everything from healthy, low-calorie meals to hearty bistro steaks and roasted salmon or trout at no extra charge."[6]

A COMMITMENT TO ANIMAL WELFARE

As a company, Blue Apron prides itself on creating healthy, ready-to-make meals for its customers. It sources most of its meal kit ingredients directly from farmers and producers. Blue Apron also states that it cares about animal welfare. The company says that its beef, poultry, and pork come from animals not treated with added hormones or antibiotics. It also follows guidelines to ensure that the animals that end up in its products are treated humanely and ethically.

NICHE SUBSCRIPTION OPTIONS

HelloFresh and Blue Apron claim a large portion of the meal kit subscription market. But there are hundreds of other companies offering similar subscription services, many of which cater to people with specialized diets. Purple Carrot offers vegetarian meal kits, with meals such as crispy brussels sprout tacos with cherry orange salsa and peanut sauce.

All the meals in Gobble's meal kit delivery service take no more than 15 minutes to prepare. The ingredients have been already chopped, peeled, and sliced. Gobble was selected as the top meal delivery kit service by *Parents* magazine because of its recipes' speedy prep time. One of its dishes is sun-dried tomato linguine in lemon-garlic butter sauce with sustainably raised ocean shrimp. Another is three-cheese lasagna rolls with butternut squash and sage brown butter sauce.

Green Chef promotes its use of high-quality, sustainable ingredients and is an option for anyone with a specialized diet, such as pescatarian, vegetarian, or vegan. Among the service's meal options is chicken and

JUST HEAT AND SERVE

Many meal kit subscription plans still involve cooking at home. But for people who just want to heat and serve, Factor75 is an option. All of its premade breakfasts, lunches, and dinners require only a few minutes in the oven or microwave, and the food is ready to be eaten. Customers can order up to 18 single-serving meals per week. "Though Factor75's recipes aren't too adventurous, there is variety," says Kelly Woo of Tom's Guide.[7]

white bean soup with cheddar cheese, sour cream, Cholula hot sauce, and tortilla chips.

Hungryroot offers a slew of options for breakfast, lunch, and dinner. Each recipe includes premade sauces, chopped ingredients, organic produce, and an optional protein. Its customers appreciate the service's customizability. "For each recipe you can substitute items (for example, if a recipe uses beef, you can swap in turkey, chicken, or a meatless alternative. You can also swap out types of noodles and other ingredients)," say writers for the website Epicurious. "It means you keep the same flavor profile even if the original recipe doesn't work with your dietary restrictions and preferences."[8]

ARTISANAL MEAL KITS

There are plenty of people across the United States who love spending time in the kitchen but are interested in branching out into new cuisines. Others don't mind grocery shopping but sometimes can't get a certain ingredient or product at their local store. Still others want to cook with their kids—or cook for just one person. For these people, there are specialized meal kit services available.

Red Velvet, a bakery in New York City, caters to people who want to learn how to make desserts. Subscribers get two kits per month, each containing a recipe and all the necessary ingredients. Consumers' favorite recipes include orange almond flourless cake, French macarons with raspberry preserves, and chocolate chip cookies.

CookUnity is a ready-to-eat meal delivery service designed for one person. There are more than 100 meal options available per week. They include a Mission-style chicken burrito and Arctic char with baby kale and spinach salad.

CookUnity works with famous chefs to come up with the recipes. "Each of CookUnity's ready-to-eat meals has a chef's name attached to it; the inference being that the chef has created the recipe you're eating at your dining table or over the kitchen counter," says Watsky. "Because this meal delivery outfit has such a wide range of options, I'd say this service is one of the best for someone with a curious palate and who likes to try new dishes. The food is all over the map, quite literally, with dozens of world foods represented, but there is consistency in quality and all of the dishes I tried were at least solid or better."[9]

Teens and kids can get in on the cooking fun too. The eat2explore service teaches kids about other countries and cultures through food with each box delivered.

FIGURES IN FOOD

OOSHMA GARG

When Gobble CEO Ooshma Garg was in college, she missed the comfort of home-cooked meals. So instead of continuing to eat out, she created a company that revolved around 15-minute meals that were simple to make, even for beginner cooks. In 2010, she launched Gobble, a San Francisco–based meal kit delivery platform. "I approached my problem not by learning how to cook and allocating all this time for myself, which I'd love to do more of now," Garg says, "but rather by automating a solution that would solve this problem, not just for me, but for everybody."[10]

Gobble began as a community where people in San Francisco could cook a delicious dish and then deliver it to someone locally for a fee. Over time, it transitioned into a meal kit service complete with all the ingredients and instructions. The journey wasn't easy. At one point, Garg was running out of money and an investor advised her to sell the business.

But she didn't give up, and in 2022, Gobble was bought by Intelligent Foods for nine figures. This made Garg the CEO of both Gobble and Sunbasket, a health-focused meal delivery company. "It might take longer, it might look different, but everybody can do anything," Garg says.[11] Garg left the company in 2023.

Every box includes recipes for three dishes; pre-prepared, nonperishable ingredients; an educational guide to a country; activity sheets; cooking tools; and more. "Adults aren't the only ones spending a lot of time in the kitchen," says nutritionist Kristy Del Coro. "Thanks to innovative cooking subscription boxes specifically designed for young cooks, more and more kids are able to learn how to prepare meals from scratch."[12]

A BOX FOR FOOD AND FAMILY FUN

When the whole family wants to get in on the cooking fun, Kidstir is an educational meal delivery subscription service that showcases a new theme each month, such as "Beach Days," "'80s Night," "Over the Rainbow," and "Winter Wonderland Cookies." Each kit comes with a shopping list, three laminated recipe cards, a cooking tool such as a spatula or measuring spoons, food-related stickers, a magazine, and a cooking-related game to play with the family. Ingredient substitution ideas are also included for people with allergies.

ENVIRONMENTAL EFFECTS

Meal kit subscription services can be a convenient and nutritional way for people to eat quality meals without spending as much time in the kitchen. But what about the effects on the environment? Shipping meal kits to millions of consumers involves cardboard, Styrofoam, plastic food trays, ice packs for perishable ingredients, and other resources. How does this compare with the environmental effects of buying food from a grocery store?

To answer this question, a group of scientists conducted a study in 2019 to compare food from five Blue Apron meal kits with the equivalent amount of ingredients purchased at a typical grocery store for similar recipes. What they found was surprising. The Blue Apron meals had a lot more packaging, but all the food provided was used, resulting in hardly any food waste. This is significant in the United States, where people throw away about 40 percent of the country's food supply every year.[13]

On the flip side, the meals in the study that were made with grocery store ingredients had less packaging but required buying food in larger amounts than necessary, which led to more waste. "Even though it may seem like that pile of cardboard generated from a Blue Apron subscription is incredibly bad for the environment, that extra chicken breast bought from the grocery store that gets freezer-burned and finally gets thrown out is much worse, because of all the energy and materials that had to go into producing that chicken breast in the first place," says Shelie Miller, an environmental scientist at the University of Michigan who led the study.[14]

Packaging and shipping individual meal kits carries an environmental cost, but in some ways it is still more efficient than purchasing the ingredients from a grocery store.

The study also showed that on average, grocery store meals produce 33 percent more greenhouse gas emissions than their equivalents from Blue Apron. "Grocery stores can't always predict demand and so generally buy more food than they can sell," explains science journalist Jonathan Lambert. "Meal kit services skip the brick-and-mortar stage altogether by shipping directly to the consumer, which cuts down on . . . distribution emissions."[15]

No matter how people acquire their food for daily consumption, there are going to be some environmental benefits and drawbacks associated with the process. It's important to weigh the pros and cons before making decisions about eating and food delivery. "Yes, plastic is bad, but it's not necessarily the whole environmental story," says Miller. "To understand the actual environmental impacts [of food production] and how to reduce them, we need to look at the whole system."[16]

CHAPTER SEVEN

UNUSUAL FOOD DELIVERY

Today it's possible to get almost anything delivered right to your door if you live in an urban area. Groceries, food subscription boxes, meal kits, and fresh meals from local restaurants are available to today's food delivery customers. But beyond these standard options, the world of food delivery has seen many offerings that are much stranger.

A BITE OF DEATH ROW

In 2008, Canadian artist Paul Kneale came up with a gruesome addition to the food delivery market. For $20, customers could order from a menu that included the last meal eaten by any death row inmate in the United States before the prisoner was put to death. In some places in the United States, these inmates are allowed whatever they would

Unusual food delivery may involve unique products, novel delivery methods, or both.

like as a final meal before their execution, and the meal selections are made public. Kneale didn't allow any special requests from customers. He also wouldn't change the meals to accommodate diets such as vegetarian or pescatarian.

For example, one meal option customers could order was the last meal of 44-year-old Charles Laverne Singleton, who was executed for murder. Singleton ate two cheeseburgers, potato salad, baked beans, fried green tomatoes, sweet potatoes, fried eggplant, doughnuts, and two vanilla milkshakes the night before he was executed in Arkansas in 2004.

"What somebody had for their last meal [is] always included in the news report of an execution," says Kneale. "[Obviously] you publish things you think people want to know about. It seemed to be a media expression of a popular desire. So, I wanted to explore that popular desire."[1]

STRANGE DELIVERY INSTRUCTIONS

In many urban areas, people who frequently use Uber Eats know they can get just about anything they need delivered, from a pack of toilet paper to steak to a platter of sushi. But sometimes customers have particularly odd instructions for their delivery drivers. One customer even included a note in their delivery order that read, "Put it in a box instead of a circle container. I refuse to eat any food if presented in a circle container. Please don't ruin my meal for me."[2]

GRILLED CHEESE FROM THE SKY

Some adventurous people have gone up in a hot air balloon to see the world from above. Other daring individuals have parachuted from a plane to see what it feels like to free-fall from high in the sky. But for most people, getting a meal delivered to the ground from above is almost unheard of—except in Melbourne, Australia.

Back in 2014, residents of Melbourne could get food delivered from the sky. A quirky dining establishment called Jafflechutes allowed customers to order grilled cheese sandwiches that floated down to them in tiny parachutes from the sky. A "jaffle" is a grilled cheese sandwich in Australia. All the customers had to do was go to a designated spot, stand there, and wait for their lunch order to float

I DIDN'T ORDER THAT

Sometimes food delivery orders go awry. They may get delivered to a neighbor by mistake. Or the wrong order might be delivered to the right house. But in February 2023, a strange thing happened in a neighborhood in Los Angeles, California. Multiple deliveries from Starbucks, McDonald's, and other fast food restaurants got dropped off at houses, though none of the recipients had ordered them. "There were chicken sandwiches, milkshakes, pastries, lattes and more," says *Los Angeles Times* reporter Daniel Miller. "Then the items started arriving multiple times a day, at all hours, delivered by Uber Eats."[3] The mystery of who had placed the orders was never solved.

The owners of Jafflechutes released the grilled cheese sandwiches and parachutes from a balcony high above the spot where the customers waited.

down to them. "We stumbled into doing Jafflechutes after a weekend at a countryside Airbnb rental without electricity or Internet," says Adam Grant, one of the founders. "Without the distraction of YouTube and video games, we spent the night talking about crazy business ideas, and by morning we had created Melbourne's first float-down eatery."[4]

CHICKENS AND EGGS

Founded in 1917, Iowa hatchery Murray McMurray delivers chickens and other birds to people's doors. There's one catch—some of the birds haven't hatched yet. The company ships soon-to-be-hatched eggs of ducks, geese, guinea fowl, turkeys, peafowl, and game birds overnight for a next-day arrival. The birds are meant to be hatched and raised for eating or for laying eggs.

For many decades, Murray McMurray Hatchery customers ordered their birds through catalogs. Today, the company's birds and equipment can be ordered on its online store. For chickens, customers can order an assorted package of rare breeds and popular ones, a package of all White Leghorn chicken eggs, or a collection of Red Star chicken eggs. The Red Star hens are brownish-red with white flecks, and the males are white-feathered with yellow skin. These hens start laying eggs at 22 weeks. People can also buy an incubator to hatch the eggs and keep them warm.

"I ordered six of Murray's Midget White turkeys along with my yearly order of a dozen layer pullets. We also added a dozen guinea keets to work on the tick population, too," says Janet Garman of Timber Creek Farm. "The birds arrived late in July after hatching and shipping. Everyone was robust and healthy! Out of all the birds, we did lose one small chick the first week. Other than that, everyone thrived."[5]

POTATO DELIVERY

Perhaps the quirkiest idea for a food delivery service comes from a company called Anonymous Potato. It delivers a

STEALING A TASTE

Every time a customer places an order for a meal, they may wonder whether the person delivering the order ever takes a bite. It turns out that some do. In 2019, restaurant food supplier US Foods conducted a survey of approximately 500 delivery drivers and more than 1,500 customers in the United States who order meals through apps such as Uber Eats, DoorDash, Postmates, and Grubhub. The study suggested that about 30 percent of drivers were sneaking a bite of the dishes they delivered.[6] In response, the food delivery companies stated that these situations were much rarer than the study found. They said they investigated any cases of missing food.

single potato. The potato can include a personal message to the gift recipient or even a photo of the recipient's face.

Optional packaged bundles include other treats such as a pop-up card, potato-themed stickers, and a handy burlap bag to hold the potato. Customers can also order additional gag gifts. These include a fleece blanket shaped like a burrito, a couch potato coffee mug, knee-high socks with french fries graphics, or a rainbow-colored tutu.

STRANGE STORIES OF FOOD DELIVERY

People getting food delivered aren't the only ones having unusual delivery experiences. Many delivery workers for Uber Eats, DoorDash, and other delivery apps have shared

Anonymous Potato recommends not eating the potatoes it sends because of the ink printed on the potatoes and potential contamination during shipping.

As with those in other public-facing jobs, food delivery workers sometimes encounter strange or unusual situations.

wild experiences they've had during their encounters with the public. One pizza delivery worker said he was greeted by 15 men in a dark room wearing cloaks and holding lightsabers when he tried to drop off their order at their dorm. They tipped him $100. "One addressed me as Master Jedi of the zaa technique. I was laughing so hard I almost dropped their drinks," he says of the surprise Star Wars–themed delivery.[7]

Another delivery driver brought ten pizzas to a basement full of middle schoolers and dozens of puppies at a puppy-adoption event. “What I didn’t expect was a gaggle of 8th-grade girls playing with DOZENS of puppies being supervised by handlers. Every kind of puppy I could imagine,” remembers the delivery driver. “I set the pizzas down on the bar and just sat on the floor and squealed and giggled while puppies tried to eat the smell of pizza off of me.”[8]

CHAPTER EIGHT

THE FUTURE OF FOOD DELIVERY

Food delivery has been a fixture of modern life for decades, and technological advances such as the internet and smartphones have transformed these services and made them more popular than ever. Since 2014, the restaurant food delivery industry has been growing 300 percent faster than dine-in sales. In 2023, online orders from restaurants made up approximately 40 percent of total restaurant sales, according to *Forbes*.[1] In that year the market size of the global online food delivery sector was estimated at more than $1 trillion, including $640 billion in grocery deliveries and $390 billion in meal deliveries.[2]

Food delivery has come a long way, but the accelerating pace of technological change means that more advances are on the way. According to the blog of delivery management platform Nash,

Many restaurants partner with multiple delivery services to reach the widest customer base possible.

By 2028, the market value of the global online food delivery industry is projected to reach $1.8 trillion.[4]

"Diners don't just prefer delivery options; they demand them. And while it may seem the market is flooded with food delivery, the food delivery business is still in its early stages. Several top trends have already emerged and continue to shape the food delivery space."[3]

CONTACTLESS DELIVERY

When the COVID-19 pandemic spread around the world starting in early 2020, stores and restaurants began offering contactless delivery to keep people safe. Contactless delivery is when a driver drops off an order at a customer's door without seeing or interacting with them. The driver leaves the order on the front porch or in a designated spot where the customer will find it. The customer then receives a text or email with a photo and receipt, confirming the order has been delivered.

Many of these no-contact practices have remained in place. "Even now, many consumers prefer contactless delivery," explains a Nash blogger. "Sometimes, you may be busy working from home, ill, or simply not dressed for the public. Some people are also immunocompromised and still want to avoid unnecessary contact."[5]

In contactless delivery, the worker may knock on the door to notify the customer that the order has arrived, then leave without interacting with the customer.

DELIVERY FROM THE SOURCE

In the days before food delivery apps, every restaurant that offered food delivery hired workers to deliver orders to customers. Then, when third-party delivery apps such as DoorDash, Uber Eats, and Grubhub came along, restaurant owners signed up in droves in the hopes of broadening their audience and getting the word out about their food. For some dining establishments, the move was a great success. But for others, the lack of control over a key part of their business in addition to prohibitive fees meant they actually lost money in the long run.

Industry experts are seeing a return to in-house delivery at some restaurants, such as Domino's Pizza. This allows

A DIFFERENT KIND OF KITCHEN

In the restaurant business, the kitchen is usually the place where the food is prepared before it's brought out to the dining room. But in the modern age of food delivery, there is a different kind of kitchen that prepares food only for delivery orders, without dine-in or takeout options. This type of kitchen, called a ghost kitchen, dark kitchen, cloud kitchen, or virtual kitchen, has a variety of benefits for restaurant owners. Start-up and staffing costs are lower, and rent is also lower because there's no need for space to accommodate dine-in eaters.

restaurants to avoid third-party fees and keep the profits for themselves. While hiring a staff of delivery workers might add more out-of-pocket expenses to their budgets, many restaurant owners think that not having to deal with the headache of partnering with third-party apps is worth it.

Restaurants that take delivery in-house can design a uniquely tailored app of their own. They can more easily incorporate rewards programs and ways for customers to provide direct feedback. Custom apps may even have a delivery tracker so consumers can see how long their orders will take to arrive at their doorstep.

"Domino's app experience is exceptional because it's tailored to their specific customer journey. There's simply no way Uber Eats, which partners with thousands of restaurants, could design a generic app that tracks each detail of the order process," says industry analyst Divya Kaushal. "Domino's is also able to take advantage of cross-selling opportunities (e.g., 'Do you want breadsticks with your pizza?') far more efficiently than the third-party apps ever could."[6]

A MEAL FROM ABOVE

In March 2024, DoorDash announced a partnership with drone delivery company Wing to test out whether it was feasible to deliver restaurant orders using drones. As part of the pilot, customers living near a specific Wendy's in Christiansburg, Virginia, could order anything off the Wendy's menu as long as the total order was under a certain weight. The company would then deploy up to three drones to make the delivery. While this was Wing's first collaboration with DoorDash in the United States, the companies had already experimented with drone food delivery in Australia in 2022. This Australian service eventually expanded to include a few dozen participating restaurants in three Queensland locations.

DRONES THAT DELIVER

Some companies, including Flytrex and DoorDash, are trying to introduce high-tech drones into the world of food delivery in select cities. There are many potential benefits to using drones for this work. Drones won't get stuck in traffic as a human delivery worker would, meaning that overall delivery time would likely decrease. Drones also cost less for restaurants to use in the long run because there is less fuel cost to consider and there isn't a roster of human delivery staff to keep on the payroll. Customers save a little money too because there's no delivery worker to tip.

However, there are also downsides to drones, such as increased clutter in the sky and unforeseen delivery delays if the drones malfunction. Still, some people and companies feel the benefits outweigh the costs. "It may sound like something out of a futuristic sci-fi movie, but it's reality, folks," says a Nash blogger.[7]

In addition to drones, some ground-based robots are beginning to make deliveries. They may even have advertising on them, bringing in more revenue to the delivery company.

CUTTING BACK ON WASTE

Food delivery has the potential to generate a large volume of waste. Unless the restaurant has made more Earth-friendly arrangements, many orders are delivered in nonrecyclable takeout containers made of Styrofoam or plastic, and those orders are carried in non-recyclable plastic bags. While some consumers do reuse these items, others just throw them directly in the trash when they're done with their meal. That means more garbage in landfills, which puts a strain on the environment.

But some restaurants are beginning to cut back on waste by not including single-use cutlery unless the customer requests it. Others are using compostable packaging and cutlery, along with bags made from recycled and plant-based materials that break down naturally in landfills. Environmentally conscious customers may start to prefer restaurants that take these steps. "Prioritizing sustainability in delivery order packaging will be a big food trend in the coming years," says a Nash blogger. "Many customers will opt for eco-friendly restaurants that make a concerted effort to reduce waste."[8]

CUSTOMIZED RECOMMENDATIONS

Customized recommendations have become an important part of marketing to consumers. This has been integrated into music services, bookselling platforms, and even clothing stores. Food delivery companies are starting to get involved too. By paying attention to consumers' buying habits, food delivery services can adjust not only the types of foods they're offering on any given day or week but also the way each user experiences ordering food for delivery. For example, if a patron regularly orders chicken curry on Sunday night for dinner, the delivery app can send notifications each time the restaurant begins offering a new curry special.

"Technological advancements have also allowed restaurants to uncover valuable assets—customer demographics and buying habits," says Kirimgeray Kirimli, a software company leader. "With 91 percent of Gen-Z consumers more likely to purchase with brands that provide customized recommendations, it's crucial for restaurants to jump on this trend. Proactively using customer data to guide a personalized marketing strategy will lead to greater customer satisfaction."[9]

INTEGRATING ADVANCED TECH

Perhaps more than any other trend, artificial intelligence (AI) is likely to play a major role in how food gets delivered. Computer systems powered by AI will get more directly involved in customer interactions. "Artificial intelligence is poised to transform ordering," says Cara Rasch of Freedonia Group, a business research company. "Imagine AI taking orders, upselling based on your preferences, and

FIGURES IN FOOD

MARC LORE

Billionaire Marc Lore, former chief executive of Walmart.com, is no stranger to new business ideas. In the 2000s, he founded Diapers.com, a diaper-delivery company for parents. His service Wonder is now transforming the food delivery experience.

Wonder launched in 2021. It soon flooded the New Jersey suburbs with cooks in vans. These workers prepared dishes by celebrity chefs such as Bobby Flay or José Andrés in customers' driveways.

By 2023, the company abandoned that idea in favor of creating brick-and-mortar food hall–style places where customers could order freshly prepared food for dine-in or takeout. They could also buy groceries or meal kits, purchase food from other restaurants, and place delivery orders on the Wonder app. Lore told the *New York Times*, "This could be the Amazon of food and beverage."[10]

Lore's full vision had not yet materialized by 2024. At that time, Wonder's locations were limited to New York and New Jersey. But he was confident the business would continue to grow.

even recommending menu items to reduce restaurant food waste."[11]

Many modern cars incorporate powerful computer systems, and food delivery companies are integrating them into the delivery industry as well. In 2021, Grubhub made a trendsetting deal with Fiat Chrysler Automobiles that enabled consumers to place a food delivery order and pay for it by using a touch screen in their vehicle. "Having a connection to Grubhub's 300,000-plus restaurants from the car provides a new line of exposure and access to those restaurants, especially with the use of the 'new favorites' feature," say Restaurant Dive reporters Alicia Kelso and Julie Littman. "If consumers are near a restaurant they have not ordered from before, they can tap a button that forwards the restaurant's menu to their email for later review."[12]

APPS AND AI

While AI seemed to suddenly take the world by storm in the early 2020s, the reality is that some food delivery apps were already experimenting with using AI to streamline their ordering and delivery processes. Uber Eats uses AI to optimize delivery routes and accurately estimate delivery times. DoorDash has AI-powered voice ordering technology that answers the calls its participating restaurants receive. Grubhub, Instacart, and Postmates all use AI in their apps as well.

FOOD DELIVERY IS HERE TO STAY

The ways people prepare and eat food are fundamental parts of how humans live, and these methods have evolved significantly over time. From medieval France to modern New York City, people all over the world have enjoyed getting food delivered. They may call restaurants on the phone, use a website on a laptop, place orders through a smartphone app, sign up for a meal kit subscription, or all of the above. Getting food delivered makes life more convenient, and there have never been more ways to do it.

In an increasingly fast-paced world, food delivery has become a much-beloved habit that is here to stay. "There is no one-size-fits-all delivery model for restaurants in today's world," says Kirimli. "However, as emerging technology continues to reshape the food delivery landscape, restaurants will benefit from embracing these advancements to stay competitive and meet the evolving expectations of today's tech-savvy consumers."[13]

ESSENTIAL FACTS

EARLY HISTORY OF FOOD DELIVERY

- Meat-delivering butchers in medieval France and meal-delivering *dabbawalas* in 1890s India were two early examples of food delivery services.
- In the 1800s and early 1900s in the United States, takeout was a convenient way for workers to pick up a meal while commuting to or from work.
- In 1922, Kin-Chu Cafe, a Chinese restaurant in Los Angeles, California, became one of the first known restaurants in US history to offer food delivery to customers.

ONLINE FOOD DELIVERY

- The online grocery delivery service Peapod was created by brothers Andrew and Thomas Parkinson in 1989.
- Launched in 1994 by Pizza Hut, the first website dedicated to delivering food to consumers was called PizzaNet. Other early delivery sites include Seamless, HomeGrocer, and Kozmo.
- In 2020, the popularity of food delivery apps for smartphones increased dramatically as the COVID-19 pandemic put a stop to in-restaurant dining.
- The top four food delivery apps in the United States are Uber Eats, DoorDash, Grubhub, and Postmates.

FOOD DELIVERY OPTIONS

- One of the most popular food delivery items in the United States has long been pizza.
- Culinary subscriptions are on the rise in the United States, offering products such as chocolate truffles, baskets of fruit, bottles of soda, and bags of coffee.
- Meal kits such as HelloFresh and Blue Apron deliver prechopped and premeasured ingredients, step-by-step recipes, and how-to photos.

THE FOOD DELIVERY INDUSTRY

- In 2023, the market size of the global online food delivery sector was estimated at more than $1 trillion. That included $640 billion in grocery deliveries and $390 billion in meal deliveries.
- Advancements such as drones, artificial intelligence, and environmentally friendly packaging are among the trends changing the food delivery industry today.

QUOTE

"Diners don't just prefer delivery options; they demand them. And while it may seem the market is flooded with food delivery, the food delivery business is still in its early stages. Several top trends have already emerged and continue to shape the food delivery space."

—*Blog for the online delivery platform Nash*

GLOSSARY

artificial intelligence (AI)
Computer systems that can learn, write, analyze, and perform other tasks associated with human intelligence.

cuisine
The cooking methods and food traditions of a particular group of people.

demographics
Specific portions of a population.

drone
A small remote-controlled flying machine.

exploitative
Taking advantage of a person, group, or situation for the purpose of profiting from it or for advancement.

fishmonger
A person or business that sells raw fish and seafood to the public.

furikake
A savory-sweet Japanese rice seasoning made from seaweed, sesame seeds, and other ingredients.

juggernaut
A literal or metaphorical force or state of being that is destructive or unstoppable and crushes whatever is in its path.

marketing
Promoting a product or service to encourage customers to purchase it.

niche
A specialized category or portion of the market for a particular kind of product or service.

pandemic
The outbreak of disease over a large area.

prohibitive
Restrictive; tending to restrain or prevent.

proprietor
Someone who is the owner of something, such as a restaurant.

reimbursement
The action of giving money back to a person to cover money that has been spent or lost.

suburb
A smaller community within commuting distance of a city.

venture capitalist
An investor who funds start-up companies in exchange for partial ownership of those companies.

ADDITIONAL RESOURCES

SELECTED BIBLIOGRAPHY

Khafagy, Amir. "Delivery Workers Are Struggling to Survive the Pandemic." *Counter*, 5 Jan. 2021, thecounter.org. Accessed 20 June 2024.

Medina, William. "A Day in the Life of a NYC Deliverista." *Streetsblog NYC*, 5 Oct. 2023, nyc.streetsblog.org. Accessed 20 June 2024.

Popper, Nathaniel. "As Diners Flock to Delivery Apps, Restaurants Fear for Their Future." *New York Times*, 9 June 2020, nytimes.com. Accessed 20 June 2024.

FURTHER READINGS

Heing, Bridey. *The Gig Economy*. Greenhaven, 2021.

Mahoney, Ellen. *Food Stars: 15 Women Stirring Up the Food Industry*. Chicago Review, 2023.

Sonneborn, Liz. *The Fast Food Industry*. Abdo, 2025.

ONLINE RESOURCES

Booklinks
NONFICTION NETWORK
FREE! ONLINE NONFICTION RESOURCES

To learn more about food delivery, please visit **abdobooklinks.com** or scan this QR code. These links are routinely monitored and updated to provide the most current information available.

MORE INFORMATION

For more information on this subject, contact or visit the following organizations:

EATER
85 Broad St.
New York, NY 10004
eater.com

Eater is a digital media brand that covers everything having to do with food and dining, including articles about food delivery and food subscription services. It has a national site, which covers food and dining culture; 23 city-specific Eater sites, which track local dining scenes; and a YouTube channel, which features short documentaries about the restaurant business.

LOS DELIVERISTAS UNIDOS WITH THE WORKER'S JUSTICE PROJECT
365 Broadway
Brooklyn, NY 11211
workersjustice.org/en/ldu

Los Deliveristas Unidos organizes and advocates for thousands of app-based delivery workers in New York City.

NATIONAL RESTAURANT ASSOCIATION
2055 L St. NW, Ste. 700
Washington, DC 20036
restaurant.org

Founded in 1919, the National Restaurant Association is the largest food service trade association in the world. It represents the needs and concerns of thousands of restaurants in the United States.

SOURCE NOTES

CHAPTER 1. BEING A DELIVERY DRIVER

1. William Medina. "A Day in the Life of a NYC Deliverista." *Streetsblog NYC*, 5 Oct. 2023, nyc.streetsblog.org. Accessed 29 July 2024.
2. Medina, "Day in the Life."
3. Bill Miller. "The 'Brotherhood' of Delivery Workers in City Seeks 'Fair Pay.'" *Tablet*, 18 Aug. 2023, thetablet.org. Accessed 29 July 2024.
4. Dashiell Allen. "A Day in the Life of a NYC Food Delivery Worker." *NYCity News Service*, nycitynewsservice.com. Accessed 29 July 2024.
5. Medina, "Day in the Life."
6. Medina, "Day in the Life."
7. Medina, "Day in the Life."
8. Winnie Hu. "Inside the Fight to Pay Food Delivery Workers $23 an Hour." *New York Times*, 8 Dec. 2022, nytimes.com. Accessed 29 July 2024.
9. Medina, "Day in the Life."
10. Hu, "Inside the Fight."
11. Medina, "Day in the Life."

CHAPTER 2. FOOD DELIVERY HISTORY

1. Emelyn Rude. "What Take-Out Food Can Teach You about American History." *Time*, 14 Apr. 2016, time.com. Accessed 29 July 2024.
2. Rude, "What Take-Out Food Can Teach You."
3. "History of Food Delivery." *Grubtech*, 2023, blog.grubtech.com. Accessed 29 July 2024.
4. Jane Holt. "Pizza, a Pie Popular in Southern Italy, Is Offered Here for Home Consumption." *New York Times*, 20 Sept. 1944, nytimes.com. Accessed 29 July 2024.

CHAPTER 3. THE INTERNET CHANGES EVERYTHING

1. Constance L. Hays. "Suburban Life in the Hectic 1990's: Dinner Delivered." *New York Times*, 20 Nov. 1992, nytimes.com. Accessed 29 July 2024.
2. Hays, "Dinner Delivered."
3. "Peapod Celebrates 25 Years as America's Leading Online Grocer." *Business Wire*, 1 Oct. 2014, businesswire.com. Accessed 29 July 2024.
4. Michael Schrage. "On-Line Pizza Idea Is Clever but Only Half-Baked." *Los Angeles Times*, 25 Aug. 1994, latimes.com. Accessed 29 July 2024.
5. Greg Bensinger. "In Kozmo.com's Failure, Lessons for Same-Day Delivery." *Wall Street Journal*, 3 Dec. 2012, wsj.com. Accessed 29 July 2024.
6. Katie Morell. "The Random Idea That Sparked a $100M Business." *American Express*, 13 May 2013, americanexpress.com. Accessed 29 July 2024.

7. "Community Highlights: Meet Ross Resnick of Roaming Hunger + RMNG." *VoyageLA*, 25 Apr. 2022, voyagela.com. Accessed 29 July 2024.

8. Jordan Hollander. "50 Online Ordering & Food Delivery Statistics." *HotelTechReport*, 23 Mar. 2024, hoteltechreport.com. Accessed 29 July 2024.

9. David Curry. "Uber Eats Revenue and Usage Statistics." *Business of Apps*, 8 July 2024, businessofapps.com. Accessed 29 July 2024.

10. Tiahn Wetzler. "Food Delivery App Boom Continues Following Lockdown-Driven Growth." *Adjust*, 2 Nov. 2021, adjust.com. Accessed 29 July 2024.

11. "Online Food Delivery – United States." *Statista*, 2024, statista.com. Accessed 29 July 2024.

12. Leah Nylen and Alexander Nieves. "As Restaurants Struggle, Cities Look to Cap Delivery Fees." *Politico*, 5 May 2020, politico.com. Accessed 29 July 2024.

13. Rachel King. "More Than 110,000 Eating and Drinking Establishments Closed in 2020." *Fortune*, 26 Jan. 2021, fortune.com. Accessed 29 July 2024.

CHAPTER 4. CONTROVERSIAL APPS

1. Shira Ovide. "Why Restaurants Are Fed Up with Apps." *New York Times*, 2 July 2021, nytimes.com. Accessed 29 July 2024.

2. Ovide, "Restaurants Are Fed Up."

3. Nathaniel Popper. "As Diners Flock to Delivery Apps, Restaurants Fear for Their Future." *New York Times*, 10 Sept. 2021, nytimes.com. Accessed 29 July 2024.

4. Popper, "Restaurants Fear for Their Future."

5. Popper, "Restaurants Fear for Their Future."

6. David Curry. "Food Delivery App Revenue and Usage Statistics." *Business of Apps*, 23 July 2024, businessofapps.com. Accessed 29 July 2024.

7. "State and Local Fee Caps for Dominant Delivery Apps." *Protect Our Restaurants*, n.d., protectourrestaurants.com. Accessed 29 July 2024.

8. Popper, "Restaurants Fear for Their Future."

9. Helen Rosner. "The Fight to Rein In Delivery Apps." *New Yorker*, 5 Oct. 2021, newyorker.com. Accessed 29 July 2024.

10. Amir Khafagy. "Delivery Workers Are Struggling to Survive the Pandemic." *Counter*, 5 Jan. 2021, thecounter.org. Accessed 29 July 2024.

11. Khafagy, "Delivery Workers Are Struggling."

12. Khafagy, "Delivery Workers Are Struggling."

13. Khafagy, "Delivery Workers Are Struggling."

14. Khafagy, "Delivery Workers Are Struggling."

15. Winnie Hu. "Inside the Fight to Pay Food Delivery Workers $23 an Hour." *New York Times*, 8 Dec. 2022, nytimes.com. Accessed 29 July 2024.

16. Hu, "Inside the Fight."

CHAPTER 5. FOOD SUBSCRIPTIONS

1. "Younger Consumers Spearhead Shift toward Subscription-Based Gifts This Holiday Season, New Survey Shows." *PR Newswire*, 19 Sept. 2023, prnewswire.com. Accessed 30 July 2024.

2. Merilee Kern, "Food and Beverage Subscriptions Surging across America." *Food & Beverage Magazine*, n.d., fb101.com. Accessed 30 July 2024.

SOURCE NOTES CONTINUED

3. "Monthly Subscription Box Expenditure." *Statista*, 2 Aug. 2022, statista.com. Accessed 30 July 2024.

4. "8 Uncommon Food Delivery Services." *Tastemade*, 2024, tastemade.com. Accessed 30 July 2024.

5. "Cookie Club." *Levain Bakery*, n.d., levainbakery.com. Accessed 30 July 2024.

6. David Watsky. "17 Best Food and Drink Subscription Gifts." *CNET*, 17 Apr. 2024, cnet.com. Accessed 30 July 2024.

7. Riddley Gemperlein-Schirm. "We Spent Months Testing Food Subscription Boxes." *Serious Eats*, 26 Feb. 2024, seriouseats.com. Accessed 30 July 2024.

8. "Real Reviews + Recommendations." *SmoothieBox*, 2024, smoothiebox.com. Accessed 30 July 2024.

9. Megan Wahn and Carina Finn. "21 Food Subscription Boxes That Make Great Gifts." *Epicurious*, 24 Oct. 2023, epicurious.com. Accessed 30 July 2024.

10. "About the Chef." *Blind Kitchen*, n.d., theblindkitchen.com. Accessed 30 July 2024.

CHAPTER 6. A RETURN TO COOKING

1. Kelly Woo. "Best Meal Kit Delivery Services." *Tom's Guide*, 22 Mar. 2023, tomsguide.com. Accessed 30 July 2024.

2. "Market Share of Leading Companies in the Meal Kit Delivery Market in the United States in 2022." *Statista*, 8 Jan. 2024, statista.com. Accessed 30 July 2024.

3. "Our Mission." *HelloFresh*, n.d., hellofreshgroup.com. Accessed 30 July 2024.

4. "Meal Kits in the U.S. – Statistics & Facts." *Statista*, 8 Jan. 2024, statista.com. Accessed 30 July 2024.

5. Alex Wilhelm. "So What Happened to Blue Apron?" *TechCrunch*, 29 Sept. 2023, techcrunch.com. Accessed 30 July 2024.

6. David Watsky. "Best Meal Delivery Services of 2024." *CNET*, 21 July 2024, cnet.com. Accessed 30 July 2024.

7. Woo, "Best Meal Kit Delivery Services."

8. Kristi Kellogg and Noah Kaufman. "The Best Meal Prep and Delivery Services 2024, Reviewed." *Epicurious*, 13 June 2024, epicurious.com. Accessed 30 July 2024.

9. David Watsky. "CookUnity Review." *CNET*, 21 Nov. 2023, cnet.com. Accessed 30 July 2024.

10. Decerry Donato. "Behind Her Empire: Gobble Founder and CEO Ooshma Garg on Finding Product Market Fit." *dot.LA*, 6 Mar. 2023, dot.la. Accessed 30 July 2024.

11. Donato, "Ooshma Garg."

12. Kristy Del Coro. "These Are the Best Kids Cooking Subscription Boxes for Young Chefs." *Spruce Eats*, 2 Sept. 2023, thespruceeats.com. Accessed 30 July 2024.

13. London Gibson. "Are Meal Kit Services Bad for the Environment, Compared to a Grocery Store?" *IndyStar*, 20 Oct. 2021, indystar.com. Accessed 30 July 2024.

14. Jonathan Lambert. "Meal Kits Have a Smaller Carbon Footprint than Grocery Shopping, Study Says." *NPR*, 22 Apr. 2019, npr.org. Accessed 30 July 2024.

15. Lambert, "Meal Kits Have a Smaller Carbon Footprint."

16. Lambert, "Meal Kits Have a Smaller Carbon Footprint."

CHAPTER 7. UNUSUAL FOOD DELIVERY

1. Jose Louren. "For $20, a Toronto Artist Delivers a Taste of Death Row." *Globe and Mail*, 27 Sept. 2008, theglobeandmail.com. Accessed 30 July 2024.

2. Liucija Adomaite and Austėja Akavickaitė. "29 of the Weirdest and Wildest Things Seen by Food Delivery Drivers on the Job." *Bored Panda*, 7 Sept. 2021, boredpanda.com. Accessed 30 July 2024.

3. Daniel Miller. "A Tasty L.A. Mystery." *Los Angeles Times*, 15 Mar. 2023, latimes.com. Accessed 30 July 2024.

4. Ben Schiller. "This Grilled Cheese Restaurant Delivers You Your Sandwich by Parachute." *Fast Company*, 29 Apr. 2014, fastcompany.com. Accessed 30 July 2024.

5. Janet Garman. "Murray's Midget White Turkey." *Murray McMurray Hatchery*, 25 Mar. 2024, blog.mcmurrayhatchery.com. Accessed 30 July 2024.

6. Dani Matias. "1 in 4 Food Delivery Drivers Admit to Eating Your Food." *NPR*, 30 July 2019, npr.org. Accessed 30 July 2024.

7. Adomaite and Akavickaitė, "Weirdest and Wildest Things."

8. Marco Vita. "The 2023 Uber Eats Cravings Report." *Uber Newsroom*, 19 Oct. 2023, uber.com. Accessed 30 July 2024.

CHAPTER 8. THE FUTURE OF FOOD DELIVERY

1. Phil Lempert. "The Future of Food Delivery Depends on Human Emotions: Not Speed." *Forbes*, 17 Feb. 2023, forbes.com. Accessed 30 July 2024.

2. Nadine Koutsou-Wehling. "Uber Eats Grocery 2024: Market Analysis." *ECDB*, 19 July 2024, ecommercedb.com. Accessed 30 July 2024.

3. "The Future of Food Delivery: Top Trends to Watch." *Nash*, 20 June 2023, usenash.com. Accessed 30 July 2024.

4. "Revenue of the Online Food Delivery Market Worldwide from 2017 to 2018, by Segment." *Statista*, 15 Feb. 2024, statista.com. Accessed 30 July 2024.

5. "The Future of Food Delivery."

6. Divya Kaushal. "Top 10 Successful Online Food Delivery Apps in the World." *Net Solutions*, 27 Jan. 2023, netsolutions.com. Accessed 30 July 2024.

7. "The Future of Food Delivery."

8. "The Future of Food Delivery."

9. Kirimgeray Kirimli. "How Technology Is Reshaping the Future of Food Delivery." *QSR*, 12 Apr. 2024, qsrmagazine.com. Accessed 30 July 2024.

10. Elizabeth G. Dunn. "He's Not Just Looking to Make a Quick Billion." *New York Times*, 10 Mar. 2024, nytimes.com. Accessed 30 July 2024.

11. Cara Rasch. "The Future of Food Takeout and Delivery." *Freedonia Group*, 2 Apr. 2024, freedoniagroup.com. Accessed 30 July 2024.

12. Alicia Kelso and Julie Littman. "Grubhub Partners with Fiat Chrysler." *Restaurant Dive*, 12 Jan. 2021, restaurantdive.com. Accessed 30 July 2024.

13. Kirimli, "Reshaping the Future of Food Delivery."

INDEX

ABOUT THE AUTHOR

ALEXIS BURLING

Alexis Burling has written dozens of articles and books for young readers on a variety of topics ranging from current events and biographies of famous people to nutrition and fitness to major milestones in history. She is also a professional book critic with reviews of adult and young adult books, author interviews, and other publishing industry–related articles published in the *New York Times*, the *Washington Post Book World*, the *San Francisco Chronicle*, and more. When Alexis lived in New York City, she got food delivered all the time. Now that she lives in Washington with her husband, cats, and hundreds of books, there are sadly only dine-in options available.